YOU'VE STARTED YOUR BUSINESS - NOW WHAT?

Five Practical Steps To Grow Your Small Business

ELLA ROSE-OJI

Spiritual Life Coach

You've Started Your Business - Now What?
Workbook

Thank you for purchasing this workbook. We created it for use with our coaching program and after several requests, decided to make it available for purchase. Please know that you are in no way obligated to participate in the coaching program.

Copyright © 2020 by Ella Rose-Ojis

Published in the United States of America
ISBN 9798627099149

All rights reserved. No parts of this book can be reproduced or transmitted in any form or by any means, electronic or mechanical, including photocopying, recording, or by any information storage or retrieval system, without written permission from Ella Rose-Oji (ojiella7@gmail.com) except for the inclusion of brief quotations.

You've Started Your Business - Now What?
Workbook

I dedicate this book to all women who have dared to step out on faith and start a business. There are many reasons why you started your businesses, all valid and all worthy. Thank you for your vision and your courage. And thanks to the ladies who took time from their busy schedules to review this book and give feedback, specifically Aminata Solammon and Elnora Bradford. I honor you and salute the Christ spirit within you. Continued blessings.

You've Started Your Business - Now What?
Workbook

TABLE OF CONTENTS

Introduction

Chapter 1   Renew Your Strength

Chapter 2   Dream Big and Write the Vision

Chapter 3   Develop a Strategic Plan

Chapter 4   Create Your Team

Chapter 5   Become Who You Need to Become

Summary

About the Author

You've Started Your Business - Now What?
Workbook

INTRODUCTION

In one twenty-four hour period three friends called to talk to me about a problem. Ranging in age from the mid-thirties to seventy, each work in a different industry and live in different states. One called to discuss her frustration related to a board meeting she chaired earlier in the day. Another friend is very frustrated with her job but is afraid to leave it to build her business. The third person not only sounded frustrated but sounded as though she had lost all hope. This was particularly disturbing because this was her third job in three years and this outcome was inevitable. Do any of these situations sound familiar to you? Over the years women have told me variations of these stories. Heck, I have experienced different versions of these stories as well. These three women share one thing in common. They are frustrated, feel stuck, and must commit to doing the work necessary to bring about the changes you want. The work involves clearing up subconsciously-held beliefs that no longer serve you which frees up energy so that you can begin to move forward. If you work through the activities in this book, I know your life will change.

The back-story, the WHY we might find ourselves in such a place is important and must be explored, but it is the HOW to do it that needs development. I want to focus on the how because if you know how, if you have a process that is simple to follow, you can tweak it as needed to move from any situation you find yourself, into a situation you would prefer to be in, and you can teach others to do the same. When you move from a place of feeling frustrated, helpless, and disempowered, you can begin to strategize.

Of the 13 million women-owned businesses in the US, African American women are the fastest-growing segment of business owners today. While 21% of these companies in the United States are owned by black women, the average black woman-owned company earned an average of $65,800 in 2019, down from 67,800 in 2014. However, the average

You've Started Your Business - Now What?
Workbook

non-minority woman-owned company earned $218,800 up from 198,500 in 2014.[1] Historically, African American women have had limited access to mainstream funding so they start low-entry businesses with limited revenue-generating potential. Many of these women start their business while still working a full-time job so they don't have the time to invest fully in their business. And often there is a lack of support from the African American community and a belief that people of other races of people won't do business with black people.

According to the same report, the number one reason African American women start a business is that they are frustrated with their jobs. These women say they can't get ahead in that they are passed over for promotions and have to train the person who is going to be their boss. The number one reason non-minority women start a business is that they want the freedom and flexibility being their own boss will give them. To change these statistics, women must first deal with why they want to start a business. Running a business is stressful enough, but to start a business out of frustration brings with it a set of beliefs and emotions that must be dealt with before you can get focused on growing your business. So you have to get clear about what you want, develop a strategy, and get to work by taking inspired actions. Change first starts in the mind, in your thinking, This workbook provides activities to help you reevaluate where you are in your thinking, reset your game plan, and get your business re-energized, moving towards the next level. I believe we live in a world of unlimited resources and unlimited possibilities and we can change this paradigm.

Self-development and self-improvement are important and necessary if you want to continue to evolve to your highest and best. And if you want to be able to move your business from a revenue of $24K to $50K, $100K or more. It's your choice. By the time you complete this book, you will have developed a written strategy to take your business to the next level-whatever the next level looks like for you.

---

[1] 2019-State of women-Owned Business Report Commissioned by American Express - Summary

You've Started Your Business - Now What?
Workbook

Once you evaluate how your business is performing financially and according to your mission, you may have some difficult decisions to make. You might decide to close your business, restructure your business, or expand your business. My goal is to help facilitate your growth and development through the decision-making process, from a spiritual perspective. This is an interactive adventure which is why a workbook format works better. To get the most value out of your sessions and your investment set yourself up for success. Be intentional and set up a schedule so that you have time to do the work. Create a space to work in. And find an accountability partner. You can only get out of this what you put into it.

There are five steps in the process. First, let's deal with the frustration by renewing your attitude. Take back your power. Most of the work is done in this step. The second step is to discover what you want; to write your vision. Step three is to create a plan to get what you want, followed by assembling the right team to help you. The final step is to work on yourself. This step is the longest because growth and development are ongoing. Now let's get started on this wonderful journey to discovery and transformation.

CHAPTER ONE

Renew Your Strength

One of the most important aspects of growth and transformation is rest and renewal. The body and mind need adequate rest to function optimally. The effects of stress on our physical bodies is evidenced by such conditions as heart disease, diabetes, and a compromised immune system. Stress also affects you mentally, making you unable to think clearly and make definitive decisions. The three women I introduced you to previously said they are frustrated. When you make a decision from a place of frustration you are not in sync with what you want to achieve or where you want to go. Instead, your energy stream is stuck in limited possibility thinking which is counter-productive to transformation and growth.

So let's go a little deeper and get in touch with what you are feeling right now. How is stress and overwhelm showing up in your life? Where is it coming from? In working with women throughout the years, I have discovered that women often don't have the words to express how they feel. They may respond, "I'm blessed" or "I'm well". I know what those

You've Started Your Business - Now What?
Workbook

words are supposed to imply, but having said those words so many times myself, I know that they often mean: "I'm so tired I don't know what to do." "My husband didn't come home again last night and I'm hurt and upset." "I don't know how I'm going to make my car payment because the money I was expecting has not come in yet." "I'm about to fall apart but I can't let you know that. " I want to keep it real if I may. Many women of color have been taught, either literally, or subliminally, to be "strong". Don't let them see you cry." "Don't let the left hand know what the right hand is doing." (That's a misunderstood quote from the Bible by the way). I understand the concept behind not telling everyone your business, or not speaking into life what you don't want to create. But when we don't take time to get real with ourselves, we sow negative seeds through our thoughts and generate negative energy, manifesting things into our lives that we don't want. When we are recognized or honored for an accomplishment we feel like an imposter because we don't think we deserve honor and recognition. Lack of self-esteem and self-confidence shows up when as a business owner you are afraid to promote your company saying, "I'm not a salesperson".

So...how are you *really* feeling? Are you feeling sad or happy? Excited or doubtful? Ashamed or proud? Regretful or satisfied that you did the best you could do under the circumstances? Are you feeling afraid, lonely, or disappointed? Or are you feeling joyful, hopeful, and expectant? Be honest with yourself and do not make a judgment about whether it is right or wrong to feel a certain way. It is important to get in touch with your feelings right now so you can put your thoughts and emotions into the right perspective. Why? Because consumers do business with people they know, like, and trust. And you are your business; your brand. If you are not operating from a good place mentally and physically, it will reflect in how you show up for your clients and customers, vendors, and business partners or associates. Whether your business is going well right now and on target with your goals and dreams or not, you need to take some time out to reflect and regroup and give yourself some love and care.

Experts in the medical and scientific community agree that people develop their foundational beliefs by the age of seven. Unless you put forth a conscious effort to change your point of view about some philosophies and concepts you may have learned. nothing will change for you. These beliefs are taught to us by parents, teachers, ministers, and others in authority over our young lives and are reset when we reach our teens as we begin to prepare to transition into adulthood. By the time we become adults and are responsible for making our own decisions, our belief patterns are firmly established. However, not all of what we believe is empowering, or still relevant. Getting in touch with why you think about your life experiences the way you do, will bring into your awareness some thoughts

You've Started Your Business - Now What?
Workbook

and perceptions that are no longer valid for who you are in your life at this moment. It may be time to let them go. As you release habits and thoughts that no longer serve you, you will become more aware of thoughts that serve you well and you can begin to walk more confidently in those truths. Do not judge yourself or anyone else. And don't start to blame anyone or anything. The goal of this activity is for you to get clarity around some issues that may be holding you back from moving to your next level. You are fine. Vow to stay open-minded to receive new truths about yourself. Once you come into alignment with what is serving you well, and what is not, it will free up energy so you can develop new beliefs that better serve you. The activity below should help you identify some areas of concern and help you identify some ways to renew your strength.

ACTIVITY

I. Identify Your Limiting Beliefs - What do you believe to be true that may no longer be your truth?

Five things I believe about myself right now are:

_____
_____
_____
_____
_____
_____
_____
_____
_____

Are these beliefs still valid?

_____
_____
_____
_____
_____
_____
_____

You've Started Your Business - Now What?
Workbook

_____
_____

How are these beliefs impacting my business (es) at this time?

_____
_____
_____
_____
_____
_____
_____

What new beliefs are coming up for you? How will they help you move forward?

_____
_____
_____
_____
_____
_____
_____
_____

II. Establish Spiritual Practices - In traditional religious practices in our communities, we are taught to worship and praise God in song and dance and prayer. We pray and ask God to solve our problems or help us solve our problems. If the problem does not get solved, we contribute it to timing, saying, "Everything in God's time." Or, "Maybe it's not meant to be." However, we are often left feeling helpless and hopeless, instead of inspired and encouraged. In this activity, I invite you to look at other practices that you may do in conjunction with praise and worship that may not only help you get clarity around your business but in other areas of your life as well.

1. Meditation - the practice of getting still and listening to hear the quiet, small voice of the Spirit as it tells you what to do next. Choose to keep this process simple. Go for a walk in

You've Started Your Business - Now What?
Workbook

the park and commune with nature. Note the sunshine as it warms your body and lights your way. Or lay in bed, and have a conversation with the Christ within and ask, "What is my next step?". What should I do now? Ask any question that you want an answer to, then wait and listen for the answer. And when the answer comes take action. Obey the prompting. My experience is that the answer may come as an idea, or someone will call me to discuss what I was meditating about, or I will feel led to take a particular action, like to watch a certain YouTube video. However, I expect to receive an answer, therefore, I get an answer. Sometimes we already know the answer but are afraid to move forward. And sometimes the answer is not the answer we want. But it is usually the best in the long run.

There are two challenges here. First, expect to receive an answer. You may have to release yourself from what you thank the answer may be and that takes courage. Sometimes the answer is to stay where you are and make no changes. That's where the second challenge arises - can I trust the answer? Know that the laws of the Universe, the word of God, will not change. The word is the law and the law... is the law. For example, Luke 6:8 says if you give, you will receive something in return, and "with the same measure it will be measured back to you ". That is scripture and it is a universal law. It just is, whether you believe it or not. When you give, you get something back, even if it is a valuable lesson learned.

I find that in African American culture trust does not come easy and I understand why. And while it may be difficult to trust a person to do what he or she agreed to do, we can trust in the principle that everything is going to work out the way it should. It might not work out the way that we wanted it to so the key is to look for the lesson to be learned or for something better than what was expected to manifest. You may not be able to control the outcome, but you can control your attitude about the outcome. And you can control your behavior - what actions you take.

Do you meditate? Why or why not? Is this a practice you could use to renew your strength?

_____

_____

_____

_____

_____

2. Affirmative Prayer - Every time we speak we make an affirmation, a statement about our lives. Affirmative prayer follows what Jesus said in Mark 11:24 about prayer- "whatever you ask for in prayer, believe that you have received it and it will be yours." There is a different level of consciousness when you ask, expecting an answer than when you ask and don't know if you will get an answer or not. Or if you ask and you don't know who the answer will come from or if you can trust the answer. Affirmative prayer assumes that because God is an omniscient spirit. He already knows what you need. When you acknowledge what you want and begin to give thanks for it in a receptive mindset, you can now begin to prepare to receive it. For example, you want to grow your business by 25% over the next quarter. You will need to put a plan into action to make this happen. You cannot control the outcome, that is whether or not your business grows by your desired amount. But you can develop a plan to make it happen, work your plan with excitement and anticipation, and acknowledge that you will appreciate any amount of growth. And if you don't get 25% this time, what did you learn through this experience that may get you closer the following quarter? You may even realize that your goal was too aggressive but now you know the amount of effort you need to maintain the growth as you continue to work towards your goal. You have free will and dominion over your life, and life may be less stressful if you change your perspective.

What is your current prayer practice? How is it serving you?

_____
_____
_____
_____
_____
_____
_____
_____
_____
_____
_____
_____
_____
_____
_____
_____
_____

You've Started Your Business - Now What?
Workbook

3. Body Movement - Exercise is a great way to restore energy. Chemically, endorphins are released when you exercise and give you an enhanced feeling of well-being. It is a natural and effective anti-anxiety treatment and it relieves tension and stress. Movement can be done through dancing, walking, yoga, tai chi, playing tennis, and swimming. I took golf lessons and would go to the driving range after work sometimes and just hit balls. I was able to enjoy the fresh air and the beautiful nature of the golf course. I had solitude because everyone out there was in their own little space. And I enjoyed having control of my time. I would leave my phone in the car or place it on vibrate in my bag so I would not be tempted to answer if someone called. Sometimes now I put on music and dance and sing as loud as I want. The idea is to change the energy around you, to separate from what is causing you to stress at the moment and put your mind on something else.

What type of activities do you, or can you start doing, to relieve stress and refocus your mind and your energy?

_____
_____
_____
_____
_____
_____
_____
_____
_____
_____
_____
_____
_____

4. Start a Journal. Sometimes you may not want to speak with someone about your problems but you just need to get your thoughts out of your head so you can process them. Journaling is a good way to do that. **Do you journal? How has it helped you? If you have not been keeping a journal, is this something you would consider? Why or why not?**

You've Started Your Business - Now What?
Workbook

_____
_____
_____
_____
_____
_____
_____
_____

5. Review Your Nutritional Habits

Overeating and under eating can be a byproduct of living a stress-filled life. I'm not talking about weight management alone but eating a nutritious meal at regular intervals. Dehydration causes multiple health issues as does making poor food choices. Most of us know what to do, we just don't make doing it a priority. During this rest and renewal period, become aware of what you are feeding your body. Keep a list of what you eat and what time you eat it for one week. You will become aware of how you are behaving nutritionally. No need to make any changes right now. Just become aware without judgment. At the end of the week, review your lists for patterns and habits that stand out. Decide which ones are good and which ones you want to change. Choose one or two habits to work on, develop a plan, and start working your plan. Commit to making small changes and be consistent. As you see progress by keeping your commitment, you will begin to see results. Then you will be inspired to create a new habit. And remember to celebrate all the successes along the way.

What steps can you take to improve your nutritional status within the next week?

_____
_____
_____
_____
_____
_____

What are some of the ways you can renew your energy and open your mind to be receptive to new ideas?

You've Started Your Business - Now What?
Workbook

_____
_____
_____
_____
_____
_____
_____
_____
_____
_____
_____
_____
_____

6. Positive Affirmation: An affirmation is a phrase or statement that you can repeat to encourage and uplift yourself. You make affirmative statements each time you speak; whether you say something true or not, positive or negative. The scripture says that the power of life and death is in the tongue. [2] This is true of the life and death of your dreams and goals unless you become aware of the conversations you are having with yourself and others.

ACTIVITY

Keep a log each day for three days of the negative statements you make. A negative statement is one that says what you don't want to show up in your life. At the end of the three days, look over the list and see how you can reframe or rephrase those statements into positive statements-what you want to show up in your life. At the end of the book is a list of affirmations to help you get started.

List three takeaways from this chapter:

_____
_____
_____
_____

---

[2] :the tongue has the power of life and death..." Proverbs 18:21

You've Started Your Business - Now What?
Workbook

You've Started Your Business - Now What?
Workbook

CHAPTER TWO

Dream Big and Write the Vision

A DJ in my hometown used to end his radio show with this sentence, "If you don't know where you're going, any road will lead you there". Now that you are refreshed, it is time to get clarity about what you want out of your life. I invite you to imagine the best possible outcome you can think of for your business. Imagine there are no obstacles in the way of you getting what you want and your business is highly successful. What problems does your business solve for people? Who are your customers? Where do they live? What is their lifestyle? How much income do they make? Who are your employees? How much money is your company generating each month and how much of that is your income from your business revenue, your salary? What charities does your business support? Doing this work now will provide valuable information when you begin working on your strategic plan.

As you begin to answer these questions. put away thoughts of lack and limitation. Allow yourself to dream as big as you can. God is no respecter of person. If one person has accomplished a goal so can you. Ask yourself: If time and money were no issue, what would I do.

You've Started Your Business - Now What?
Workbook

ACTIVITY: The Wheel of Life

1. Take a clean sheet of paper and draw a big circle in the center. Or use the wheel on the next page.
2. Divide the circle into 10 sections, like a large pie.
3. Outside of each section write one of the following categories: Wealth/Finances, Health, Family/friends, Health, Relationships, Personal Growth, Spirituality, Career/Business, Physical environment, Community Involvement
4. For each category ask yourself: On a scale of 0 - 10, 10 being the highest level of satisfaction, where am I? Write the number inside the wedge. Then ask yourself, where am I now and write in that number. For example, I want to be at a ten in health but you feel you are at a 5 because you are not at a weight you'd like to be at and are not eating healthily. In the health wedge, you would write 10 at the top and 5 in the middle. Do this for each section that is important to you right now.
5. After reviewing each section, look at the areas where you did not score ten and choose 1 or 2 areas you would like to make some changes in.
6. Ask yourself, Why did I give myself this score? What do I need to do to get to the next level in this area? Complete for each category you have chosen to work on in Step 5.
7. Begin to develop goals and an action plan to reach the goals. Pray, meditate and for divine guidance and direction, and affirm the outcome you want in each category.

Scoring Key:

8 - 10 Very Satisfied

5 - 7   Reasonably Satisfied but this may be an area to explore ideas to move up a level.

0 - 4   Not Satisfied and need to look at ways to enhance satisfaction in this area.

You've Started Your Business - Now What?
Workbook

WHEEL OF LIFE

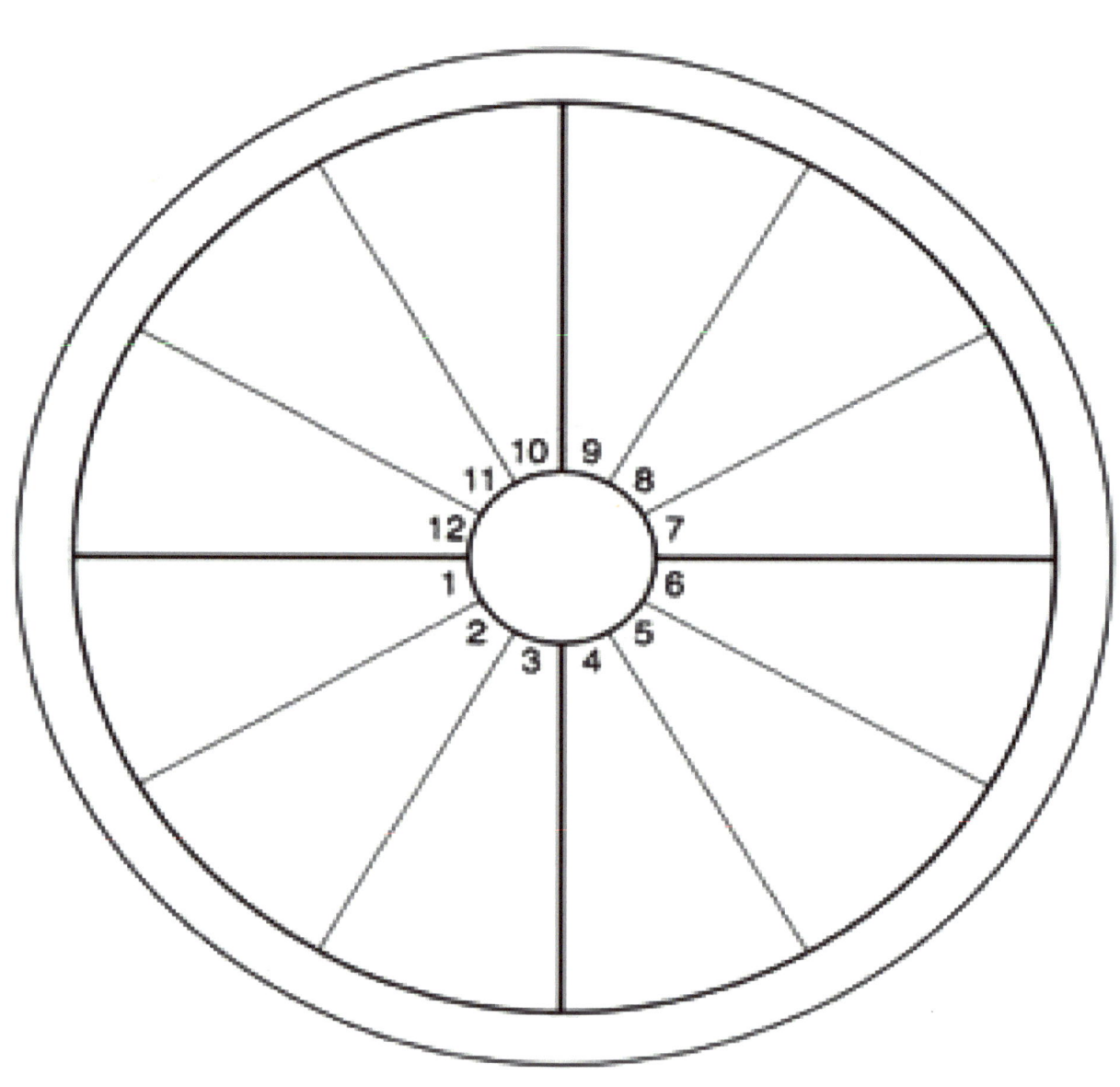

You've Started Your Business - Now What?
Workbook

ACTIVITY

Write Your Vision

Creating a tangible vision of what you want for your life and your business is one technique that helps imprint your desires onto your business and in your life. Use your imagination to create a vision board below. The only limitations in life are those that we create in our minds. Everyday, people manifest and do the "impossible". Dream about what is the highest and best for you, your family, and your business. What do you want to accomplish for your family? Allow your imagination to run wild. Know that you are surrounded by a divine energy (God, Spirit, Universe) that is goodness and there is an unlimited supply of everything you need available to you when you are ready to receive it. Expect that when you ask for something you will receive it or something greater than you expected. And when you give you will get something in return. These are Biblical truths and Universal laws.

You've Started Your Business - Now What?
Workbook

Plan - Organize – Direct - Control

(Seek – Knock – Ask)

Begin thinking about your goals and the steps you need to take to prepare to reach them.

Specific Goal	Measurable	Actions Needed	Relevant	Time Oriented

You've Started Your Business - Now What?
Workbook

Thoughts and Ideas

As you begin to dream and envision your new reality, ideas and thoughts will begin to show up for you. Write them down. Don't try to analyze them at this time, just write them down so you don't forget them. You can review them later and decide if they require further study or action.

_____
_____
_____
_____
_____
_____
_____
_____
_____
_____
_____
_____
_____
_____
_____
_____
_____
_____
_____
_____

You've Started Your Business - Now What?
Workbook

CHAPTER THREE

Develop a Strategic Plan

Now that you have completed the vision for your business, it's time to develop a strategic plan to make it happen. There is a difference between a business plan and a strategic plan. A business plan is a requirement if you want to get funding. It may be difficult to get data when you first start your business so you may have to rely on general information and estimated financial projections of businesses like yours. But after the first year or so you will have data specific to your company. Then you can update the plan with real-time data. If you haven't written a business plan for your business I suggest you take the time to do it now. It can be as detailed as you feel you need at this time. Fortunately, there are many resources available to help you, including the local Small Business Development Center or Chamber of Commerce. Review it at least annually.

A strategic plan is a type of business plan that is used for long term planning and growth, usually three to five years. Your vision board will be a source of information as you begin to create a plan to get your business to the next level. Before you start creating or updating your strategic plan, perform an honest assessment of where your business is now. Some questions to answer are listed in Chapter Two.

Many things can happen along the way to your end goal, but failure is not one of them. Napoleon Hill said failure is when your plan doesn't work. It is a temporary defeat and an indication that you need to review your plan and make adjustments. YOU are not a failure.

You've Started Your Business - Now What?
Workbook

Your plan will take some work. Some challenges may happen on the way to achieving your goals. You may even change your mind and decide this is no longer what you want. That's okay. But here are five steps to follow to help with this process.

Step one - Stop procrastinating.

Step two -Make a decision. Be intentional. Decide to create a plan for your business. If you already have a plan, pull it out and review it. If you have a team, employees, or other stakeholders, invite them to participate in a planning session. You may discover their input to be informative and it is a way to let them know that you value their input.

Step three - Create the plan. It can be one page or many pages. You decide. Ask for help if you need to. The plan is a roadmap, a guide to help you get to your next destination.

Step four - Implement the plan. Put it into action.

Step five - Be persistent. Review your plan quarterly or as often as necessary to make sure you are on track. It may be to your advantage to develop a good plan with a few steps and enlarge the plan as the business grows and develops.

About your business:

1. **What problem does my business solve for my client? What transformation does my company help my clients facilitate?**

_____

_____

_____

_____

_____

_____

2. Why does my company do better than other companies? What is my unique proposition?

_____
_____
_____
_____
_____
_____

3. Are my products or services priced correctly? Do I feel honored when I give a quote? Do I feel I am honoring my client with my prices? Am I honoring myself?

_____
_____
_____
_____
_____
_____
_____

Note: No one can ever pay you what your time is worth. But you can expect to be paid for the outcome or results you give the client. Know the results you can give your customer and be able to express that result confidently.

You've Started Your Business - Now What?
Workbook

CHAPTER FOUR

Create Your Team

Not one of us can do it all alone. Regardless of your business model, you will need help at some point. There are team members that are essential to running a business and may include a tax preparer or accountant at a minimum. You may work with independent contractors or have employees who work for your company. Your team may also include vendors, social media managers, coaches, and mentors. You decide who you need on your team based on the skills you need to operate your business efficiently and effectively, your strategic plan, and the goals you are trying to reach with your business. While completing this activity, think about what kind of help you will need in the short term as well as in the long run. Then, as you are networking and building relationships, you will be aware when you meet someone who might be able to help you later.

Managing people can be challenging. Learn to set boundaries, to prioritize, and to delegate and follow up. I think these skills are foundational if you are a business owner. If you don't have these skills, I suggest you learn them. They will help prevent some stress and frustration as your business grows.

You've Started Your Business - Now What?
Workbook

ACTIVITY

1. What skills are needed to be successful in your business? Make a list of your skills, strengths, and weaknesses. Then make a list of the skills and personality types you will need to grow your business to the next level.

_____
_____
_____
_____
_____
_____
_____
_____
_____

2. What are the key roles/positions you oneed to fill in your business based Question #1?

_____
_____
_____
_____
_____

3. How will you attract these people to your business? What's in it for them?

_____
_____
_____

4. Your clients are probably the most important part of your team. How will you get new clients for your business?

You've Started Your Business - Now What?
Workbook

_____
_____
_____
_____
_____
_____
_____

How will you take care of the clients that you already have?

_____
_____
_____
_____
_____
_____
_____
_____
_____

> "Where two or three are gathered together in my name (who believe), I am there with them." Matthew 18:20
>
> Teamwork creates synergy and stimulates creativity and learning.
>
> Working together builds trust.
>
> I am so happy and grateful for beneficial and synergistic relationships.

You've Started Your Business - Now What?
Workbook

CHAPTER FIVE

Become Who You Need To Become

Many of you say that your business is your ministry. I assume you mean that you were spiritually led to provide the services or products you offer. If this is true, you have a responsibility to operate your business from the highest level of consciousness, to be intentional, and to generate the revenue you need to accomplish the mission of your business. And this is the expectation of your employees, vendors, customers, everyone that you come into contact with. They should be able to see the mission being carried out in the way you do business; how you treat your customers and other team members, and from the feedback you get about your goods and services.

Core values are beliefs and principles that guide your behavior, influence how you interact with others, and dictate what you believe to be true in your daily life experiences. In the introduction, I stated that this book is more about the HOW than the WHY. Well, this section is more about the WHY. Why do you think the way you do? The short answer is

You've Started Your Business - Now What?
Workbook

because you were programmed to. Most people are still operating from what they were taught as young children. They repeat phrases and mantras that were taught to them by well-meaning parents and grandparents, preachers, teachers, neighbors, the news media, and many other sources. They form an opinion based on a negative event or a positive event that they experienced and that opinion influences how they deal with that situation for life. Sadly, many people never take time to examine whether what they believe is true or not. It might have been true for what they were experiencing at the time, ten, twenty, or thirty years ago. It might be true for what you experienced in your past. But is it still true for you today? In the now?

Core values for your business serve the same purpose and are usually spelled out in your mission statement or a values statement. Core values can be positive such as a belief in being a good steward of company resources, or negative, such as being greedy and focused on lack and survival.

What are your core values? Do you have a personal mission and vision statement for you personal life and your business? Are they congruent with how you see yourself running your business?

_____
_____
_____
_____
_____
_____

How do express your core values in your relationships and decision making?

_____
_____
_____
_____
_____
_____

You've Started Your Business - Now What?
Workbook

What are your natural gifts? What are you exceptionally good at doing and what skills do you struggle with?

_____
_____
_____
_____
_____
_____
_____

What self-development and self-improvement activities are you involved in? What is the last book you read and why? What are your key takeaways and do they require you to take some type of action?

_____
_____
_____
_____
_____
_____
_____
_____

What is your plan for networking and meeting new people? Do you know how to start a meaningful conversation with a "stranger"?

_____
_____
_____
_____
_____

You've Started Your Business - Now What?
Workbook

_____
_____

What characteristics are you working to develop? For example, self-confidence, joy, peace, forgiveness, spiritual understanding, persistence, consistency?

_____
_____
_____
_____
_____
_____
_____

What does failure mean to you? Describe how you process and deal with this concept.

_____
_____
_____
_____
_____
_____
_____
_____
_____

Note: Sometimes memories come up that cause you pain, sadness, anxiety, anger, or fear. Please reach out for help if you need it.

You've Started Your Business - Now What?
Workbook

SUMMARY

Let's revisit the three friends that I introduced to you at the beginning of the book. I have spoken with each of them within the last week and only one of them said she was ready to make some changes in her life. The other two began the conversation right where they left off last time. They have taken no action to change the situation they are in. This book is not a business how-to book. There are many resources available specific to your business model and the industry you are in to help with specific issues. The purpose of this book is to help you get mentally and spiritually prepared to transform your life and your business. Everything that is created begins with a thought. What you focus on not only grows, it expands as well. Most people separate their spiritual beliefs from their business goals, except to pray when they get in trouble. The five steps discussed in this book can be used in any area of your life and allow you to be proactive and operate from an empowered position of strength. I urge you to be a doer. These principles will work if you put them to work and are the answer to HOW. Repeat these steps periodically so that you can stay aware of what is happening currently, and you can also predict and plan for the future.

The IRS and other government agencies set the criteria that determine what makes an entity a business. You set the criteria for what determines whether your business is successful or not. Be aware of what other businesses like yours are doing and how they are performing because it makes good business sense. But don't compare yourself to them and don't compete with them. Determine what success looks like for your business. Set standards of performance and service and develop a process to monitor how it measures up to your vision. Know your market and the benefits that your product or service offer in the marketplace and serve your clients and customers with a spirit of love and excellence.

My background is nursing and healthcare and my eventual goal was to own a top of the line skilled nursing facility and adult daycare center. Many things happened in my life and I never opened a facility or daycare center. Not because it wasn't a great idea, but because I

You've Started Your Business - Now What?
Workbook

never developed a definitive plan to do so. Of course, I learned this through reflection and introspection and I say this in retrospect. However, as an entrepreneur, I have owned several other businesses. and I never considered either a failure. I learned valuable lessons in each venture. I have also worked with several business models including network marketing, product manufacturing, and sales, publishing, consulting, and coaching. These businesses work well with my personality, my skill set, my energy level, and my core values. My goal in life is to be the best version of myself that I can be and to provide the best service I can provide through my business ventures. And at the end of the day, I want to operate from a clear conscience with a sense of peace and joy over my life. As you work through the activities in this workbook, you should develop this kind of clarity around who you are and who your business is. This is your brand.

First, take time to rest and regroup. You can do this through prayer and meditation, exercise, and proper nutrition. Prevention is the best plan so create a habit of renewing your mind and body periodically. It doesn't need to cost much money to do this. A walk in the park may cost nothing.

Second, evaluate where you are at the present moment concerning where you want to be. Are you living your dreams? Is your vision unfolding as you imagined? How do you feel about how your business is going right now? Do not judge or blame anyone or any set of circumstances. Just become aware of how your business is performing as compared to how you expect it to be performing. You may need to do some forgiveness work here.

Third, review your business plan and your strategic plan. Revise if needed. If you don't have a written plan for how to move your business forward, take the time to develop one now.

Fourth, decide if you need some new team members. You may need to reassign some employees, offer additional training, or recruit some new people. As you bring people on board, do your due diligence to figure out who would be the best fit for the position. Are their core values in alignment with the core values of the company?

You've Started Your Business - Now What?
Workbook

Finally, evaluate your personal life outside the boundaries of your business. Sometimes we get so caught up in life experiences that we forget who we are. This is especially true for women who are expected to play so many roles, to be strong and not complain, and to be ready to help others solve their problems at the drop of a hat. One day you realize that you don't know who you are as a person anymore. You can't enjoy your success. You may feel like an impostor. It is usually this stage that will lead you to the first step-rest and renewal. And the cycle repeats itself.

Remember that nothing will change for you unless you make a decision to change it and take the necessary actions to bring the change about. You are not alone and you don't have to go it alone. The universe has already assigned someone to help you once you ask for help. Pray, but when you pray move your feet.

Finally, always express thankfulness and gratitude for every experience, whether you think it is positive or negative, good or bad. To paraphrase Napoleon Hill, in every seed of adversity is an equal or greater benefit. Grow from your experiences. Bless it, and keep moving forward.

You've Started Your Business - Now What?
Workbook

AFFIRMATIONS[3]

- I radiate success. My body is healing and full of energy.

- I eat well, exercise, and get plenty of rest.

- I greet today with the anticipation of the good God has prepared for me.

- It is not too late for me.

- I am a walking word from God! Glory to the Christ within me.

- Everything I do is fun, healthy, and exciting.

- I attract new clients every day.

- My positive attitude, confidence, and hard work naturally draws new opportunities to me.

- My workplace is peaceful and full of love.

- I am so happy and grateful now that money flows to me from multiple sources, in increasing amounts on an ongoing basis.

- Every day in every way, I am getting better and better.

---

[3] blog.mindvalley.com/positive affirmations

ABOUT THE AUTHOR

"And you shall know the truth and the truth shall set you free." John 8:32 (KJV)

Ella R Oji is a proud Mother, Grandmother, Great-grandmother, author, and serial entrepreneur. A retired Registered Nurse, she has spent her life helping people in one capacity or another. In recent years she realized the magnitude of what she does when several people reached out to her to thank her for how she had helped them through some rough times in their lives. Ella decided to become intentional and enrolled in a coaching program to learn some professional skills. In the meantime, she was experiencing a spiritual transformation which enabled her to get clarity around her beliefs and principles. Using the steps discussed in this book she has rebranded her life at different stages of her life as she has evolved through the years. At seventy-two years old the best is still yet to come.

A native of Georgia, she currently lives in Memphis, TN, and is a member of Unity Christian Church of Memphis.

You've Started Your Business - Now What?
Workbook

Other books by this author: Available at www.amazon.com/dp1698167970 in paperback and on Kindle

Caring For Your Skin - Naturally is designed to answer the question: "What exactly is a natural product?" Consumers are told to read the label to gather information about the product. But if you don't understand what the ingredients in the product are used for you will not be able to understand whether the product will provide the solution you are looking for. This book includes a chart that lists the most common ingredients used in bath and body care products today. Most of them are synthetically produced and have been identified as having health or safety risks. Once you are familiar with them however, you will be better prepared to read the label and empowered to make better purchasing decisions.

Additionally, there is a list of common ingredients used in natural products. You will be able to compare these ingredients to ingredients listed on the labels of commercial products. This information will be helpful if you decide that you want to make your products.

For more information: www.eumerose.com

Follow us on www.facebook.com/eumerose and at www.instagram.com/eumerose2